Dream
Rooms
for
Real
People

Decorating Den's

Dream Rooms for Real People

Award-Winning Makeovers for Every Room in Your House

Carol Donayre Bugg, ASID, DDCD

ACROPOLIS BOOKS LTD.
WASHINGTON, D.C.

ACROPOLIS BOOKS LTD.
11250-22 Roger Bacon Dr.
Reston, VA 22090

Attention: Schools and Corporations
ACROPOLIS books are available at quantity discounts with bulk
purchase for educational, business, or sales promotional use. For
information, please write to: SPECIAL SALES DEPARTMENT,
ACROPOLIS BOOKS LTD., 11250-22 Roger Bacon Dr.,
Reston, VA 22090.

**Are there Acropolis books you want but cannot find in your
local stores?**
You can get any Acropolis book title in print. Simply send title and
retail price. Be sure to add postage and handling: $2.25 for orders
up to $15.00; $3.00 for orders from $15.01 to $30.00; $3.75 for
orders from $30.01 to $100.00; $4.50 for orders over $100.00.
District of Columbia residents add applicable sales tax. Enclose
check or money order only, no cash please, to:

      ACROPOLIS BOOKS LTD.
      80 S. Early St.
      Alexandria, VA 22304

Library of Congress Cataloging-in-Publication Data
Bugg, Carol Donayre, 1937–
    Decorating Den's dream rooms for real people : award-winning
    makeovers for every room in your house / Carol Donayre Bugg.
       p. cm.
     ISBN 0-87491-958-4 : $29.95
     1. Interior decoration.   I. Decorating Den Systems.   II. Title.
NK2110.B83   1990
747—dc20   89-18647
                                                   CIP

Art Direction and book design by Kathleen K. Cunningham
Penelope Kriese, design assistant

Printed in Singapore

Dedication

This book is dedicated to all of the Decorating Den interior decorators who are bringing beauty, comfort, and good design to the homes of people all over the world.

With Special Appreciation

The inspiration for *Dream Rooms For Real People* comes from a contest held for the interior decorators of Decorating Den Systems, Inc., an international franchise company. Once a year their talented decorators are invited to submit presentation boards to the Dream Room contest showing designs they have created to solve their customers' problems.

In recent years as Decorating Den grew to a thousand franchisees and contest participation increased, the Dream Room entries were taken to New York to be judged by the editors of national women's and home fashion magazines. Contest boards cover every room in a house with a special category for window treatments. Comparing the "before" pictures and description of the customer's needs and desires with the decorator's solution and "after" photos reveals stunning makeovers.

My husband and I began our involvement with Decorating Den five years ago. From the outset, I have been impressed with the talent and quality of work associated with this company. About the time I began thinking of compiling the Dream Room entries into a book, I met Kathleen Hughes, now the publisher of Acropolis Books Ltd. Kathleen showed interest in including us in a chapter of a book she was planning. After Kathleen saw our contest boards the chapter was turned into a book, and *Dream Rooms For Real People* was conceived.

Thank you, Kathleen, for your advice and encouragement these past two years. My sincerest appreciation to all the magazine editors who have participated in the Dream Room contest, and most especially to D. J. Carey, Home Design Editor of *1001 Home Ideas.* D. J. has always been a faithful supporter of Decorating Den, and has honored us by writing the foreword to *Dream Rooms For Real People.*

I want to thank the Decorating Den interior decorators who took the time and energy to enter the Dream Room contest . . .

without them this book would not have been possible. One of the most fun parts of putting the book together was interviewing the customers. They were a joy to talk to, and in every instance they had wonderful stories to tell. My heartfelt gratitude goes to Patti Coons, Decorating Den's Director of Communications, for turning the Dream Room contest into a major event, and for her continuous support and inspiration.

To my husband and partner, Jim . . . for inspiring and motivating me to write this book . . . I thank you. For your enthusiasm, optimism, vision, warmth, love, and for the extraordinary time we have shared . . . I love you.

Table of Contents

Foreword

As a new homeowner, I am overwhelmed with decisions and ideas for decorating our 19th-century farmhouse in Connecticut. A day doesn't go by that I don't clip a page from a magazine (me! a magazine editor) or send away for catalogues. I call it my reference pile. Months have gone by, the reference pile now fills a small room upstairs. But I still haven't made a decision about our house. I can't seem to commit myself to one idea, one color, or even one style for a dining room table.

What really troubles me is that my training and experience as a decorating editor doesn't make my decision any easier; in fact, it makes it harder. I suffer from the notion that there will be a better solution to my decorating dilemma or that there will be a prettier fabric or a fresher color. Too many choices paralyze me! My only comfort is that friends who are designers also find it difficult to undertake projects in their homes.

Decisions are tedious when decorating your own home because it's too emotional and you can't be objective. It's as if you know your house too well. In fact, so well that you no longer can see why you were attracted to it in the first place. All you see are the negatives which seem overwhelming and unsolvable. Only an impartial, creative, and talented decorator can pull you out of your decorating despair.

Like a magician, a decorator pulls things out of the air: some color chips, a few fabric swatches, a special piece of furniture mixed all together and voila! you have a dream room.

It is with their magicians' eyes that decorators discover wonderful architectural features to highlight, an accent color that you never imagined, a refurbished piece of furniture that was destined for the dump. It certainly is magic when your decorator opens the door to that room that made you wince and suddenly it looks better than any of your clippings. Now you realize why you bought this house in the first place.

A few years ago, I was asked to judge the Dream Room contest sponsored by Decorating Den. I remember the prospect of judging hundreds of entries. After a few hours of poring over these rooms, I was certainly impressed—not only had these decorators magically transformed rooms, but did so for all types of assignments, both large and small.

As you read this book you will probably recognize some of your own decorating dilemmas and how they were solved. Seeing our problems solved in someone else's home gives us strength to address our own problems. In fact, since working on this piece, I have ragged my bedroom walls, chosen fabric for our guest bedroom, and even worked up the nerve to paint our kitchen apple green. So go ahead, read and then take some action. It'll be more fun than you ever thought.

Deborah James Carey
Home Design Editor
1001 Home Ideas

Introduction

There are as many visions of what a dream room is as there are individuals. Whether it's warm and cozy, luxurious and romantic, or light and airy, each dream room reflects the feeling its owner would like that room to have. When you think of the time, energy, and money that decorating takes, such a room might seem like an unattainable dream, but in reality your dreams can come true.

Dream Rooms For Real People is a collection of stories of people, like you, who have their own personal lifestyles, their own unique taste, their definite color preferences, and their particular budget constraints. All are people who have the same concerns as you about where to begin and how to work around what they already have. When they began their decorating projects, they, too, felt apprehensive. But now, as they reflect back, they ask themselves, "Why did I wait so long?"

The majority of interior decorating books on the market today concentrate on a particular style or region. Others narrow their content to special areas of a home. Still others have a signature look associated with certain companies or designers. What makes *Dream Rooms For Real People* unique in the world of decorating books is the scope of interiors shown.

Every area of a home is included . . . luxurious master bedrooms, inviting living rooms, comfortable family rooms, super kitchens and breakfast areas, lovely bathrooms, and special rooms for very special people. There is even a chapter on window wizardry. All styles of decorating are covered . . . traditional, contemporary, transitional, eclectic, country . . . French, English, Oriental, and, of course, all periods of American. You will also find a vast array of color schemes . . . from very colorful to serenely monochromatic.

What you see in *Dream Rooms For Real People* are homes from coast to coast, north to south, where the size of rooms and decorating budgets ranges from modest to grand or falls somewhere in between. You will find rooms decorated for everybody, from the newborn baby, to the teenager, to the first home buyer, to all the rooms in a woman builder's own home, to an "eightysomething" couple who are still redecorating. What you find in *Dream Rooms For Real People* is no one distinct look, style, or period, nor any glaring color statements. What you will discover is a decorating book devoted to individuality.

Beauty is in the eye of the beholder. Each room reflects the taste and personality of the person or people living there. By looking at the before pictures of each room, you'll learn about the different challenges their owners faced. Then you'll be able to relate your own decorating situations to some of those faced here. Picture yourself resolving your decorating problems as they did, and enjoying your own stunning makeovers that will provide you daily joy and comfort.

Chapter 1

Decorating Your Home

Dispelling Decorating Myths

Do you still believe that . . .

you have to spend a small fortune?
you have to start from scratch?
you have to do all your rooms at the same time?
you have to decorate your master bedroom last?

Affordable Decorating

Years ago it was true that only the wealthy could afford to decorate. But with the advent of man-made products and mass production techniques affordable decorating became possible. Now the home furnishings industry offers unlimited choices of colors, styles, and materials in all price ranges.

Your Home Is You

In the past it was common to be told that you had to get rid of your old furnishings and start from scratch. Nowadays, however, people will no longer be dictated to. In fact, the charm and sentiment of what you already have gives character and personality to your home.

One Room at a Time

People often think that because they are not ready to redecorate their entire home, perhaps they should wait and not do anything. It *is* better to have a plan for your whole home, but you can begin by doing one room at a time.

Treat Yourself

Because your bedroom isn't often seen by guests, it becomes the most overlooked area in your home. Yet, it's the room where you spend a great part of every day. Why not make your master bedroom your top priority? Treat yourself to a luxurious retreat that will restore and revitalize your spirit.

Where Do You Begin?

Like all first steps, turning your dreams of a beautifully decorated home into a reality begins with making the decision to do something about it. Once you overcome the mental obstacle to change, you're on your way.

Start by taking stock of what you already have, and make an honest appraisal of what you want to keep. Beware of building your new decorating scheme around something you inherently dislike. You're better off selling the mistake or even giving it away.

If you're not quite sure what your style and color preferences are, do what many of the people did whose rooms are shown in *Dream Rooms For Real People*. Clip pictures out of magazines, and over time, you'll begin to see a pattern develop that will help you define the look you want for your home.

Color Impact

Color is the most important element in decorating; it can make or break a room. Agreeable color combinations can unify the most diverse elements in a room. Often, when you know there's something wrong but can't quite put your finger on it, it's the result of clashing colors. The simple elimination of an outdated or jarring color can restore a room's harmony. Even more effective is introducing a new color that unifies all of the various elements.

Everyone has a degree of color sensitivity, but a word of caution. It's easy to fall into the trap of saying that you don't like a particular color, only to discover that when you say you hate green you're thinking avocado, like our Florida master bedroom remodeler, Joy Butler. Keep an open mind when you are deciding on your color palette.

One of the best ways to learn which colors go together is by studying the harmonious color relationships that you find in great works of art, in nature, and in fabric and wallpaper patterns.

Mixing Prints and Patterns

A print fabric is a good starting point for a color scheme that will breathe new life into a stale room, or set the tone for a new look. Decorating with a lively floral, a vibrant stripe, or a sharp geometric print can bring a revitalized look to a humdrum room or it can create a new decorating direction.

Mixing and matching prints and colors can make a room vital, but combining them skillfully takes a trained eye. The trick is how you treat the different scales of the patterns and how you coordinate colors.

Surrounding Yourself in Beauty

The selection today of wallcoverings is mind boggling. One of the redecorators included here, Virginia Sutherland, said, "I used to think that I didn't like wallpaper. What I didn't like was looking through all of those wallpaper books." Any design, theme, or color can be found in one of the hundreds of books produced yearly. What looking through them takes is a lot of patience, some help, or a combination of both.

The labor of hanging wallcovering can be more than half the cost of the project. While I do not recommend doing it yourself, it is possible to save money preparing walls, as did Joan Calcaterra and her sons in their Chicago home. But, in most instances, money spent on professional measuring and installation will be one of your most valuable investments. Sometimes it even saves marriages.

Laying the Groundwork

When building or remodeling, one of the most difficult decisions is selecting hard flooring products. Whether to go with hardwood or tile, slate or resilient, and then deciding on stain or color, and the pattern or design are hard choices to make because once the flooring is in place it is not easy to change. Taking the time to research the various products will be helpful in making a final decision.

Carpeting

Plush wall-to-wall carpet can provide lush color and texture to any room in the house, and with today's various stain retardants, carpet means easy maintenance. Besides giving a room a luxurious feeling, when the same color carpet is used throughout a house, it visually expands and ties all of the rooms together.

Area rugs are used to accent and define space within a room. exotic Orientals and dhurries, sculptured and bordered, and custom patterned and colored rugs add an important decorative element to a room. There are many examples throughout the book that show the effective use of area rugs, such as the elegant mum design of Marian Welch's custom living room rug.

Furniture Style

Most people live with an eclectic mixture of furnishings. Pieces brought from other homes and previous lifestyles are mixed with new furniture. Some rooms make a style statement, such as the Dellorfanos' French master bedroom or William Chesley's traditional 18th-century living room. Whether a room is of a definite period, or is a blending of various eras, comfort and livability are of the utmost importance.

Upholstered pieces of furniture, because of wear and tear, are generally the first to be replaced. Besides, there's nothing like the colors and pattern of a new fabric on a sofa or chair to rejuvenate and update a room. For an example of this, see Alice B. Newsome's sparklingly renewed living room. Wingback, tightback, or camelback, multi-pillowed, roll-armed, or skirted, there is an upholstery style to fit every lifestyle.

Pulling It All Together

Pulling it all together means adding the finishing touch with accessories. Think of dressing your room the way you dress yourself. Adding jewelry, hose and shoes, belt and handbag, personalizes your outfit. With the appropriate lamps and pictures, pillows and flowers, and with your special collections and mementos, you give your rooms that individual touch, such as those in the Tebos' dining room.

Lamps not only make beautiful accents, they can give us both mood and task lighting. If you are looking for a quick update for a room, consider replacing your large drum shades with newer, smaller-scaled and tapered shades. Wall and floor lamps free up tabletop space, and are usually adjustable for your convenience. Good examples are those in the Sunrise...Sunset master bedroom.

Accessorizing is not a one-time thing; it's something that is constantly evolving and changing. Part of the fun is building collections, as did Linda Risley, who has a kitchen full of copper pieces she has found all over the world. Beautiful and meaningful accessories add panache and create rooms with your own distinct look.

Real Dream Rooms

The range of interior decorating shown in *Dream Rooms For Real People* varies as much as the locales across the country. In some instances a room has been completely redecorated, but more often, it has been the addition of a new fabric or updated color, or changing the window treatment that has brought new life to a room.

From small to large, from new to lived in to remodeled rooms, with large or modest budgets, all of the rooms have one thing in common. They are the unique expression of the lifestyle of the people who live in them. The feeling of renewal that comes from redecorating was best expressed by Joan Rudloff, whose bedroom and living room are featured in this book: "I never really felt that good about any of our rooms. Now, no matter what has happened to me during the day, when I come home I feel uplifted by the beauty and comfort that surrounds me."

Chapter 2
Nashville Notable . . . A Small Gem of a House

By not playing it safe, former "American Magazine" TV host, Jan Snider, saved her small Nashville house from becoming a bland flop, and turned it into a dramatic hit instead. She was preparing to go with soft, muted colors (because everyone said they would make the rooms look larger) when an impulse purchase of a sumptuously scaled navy leather sofa led her to change her color course. Whatever the rules might be, Jan knew that she and her husband, Terrell McDaniel, preferred deep, rich colors.

There were two other major considerations in setting the decorating stage. The open floor plan of this one-story house, where each room can be seen from the others, and Jan and Terrell's eclectic collection of furniture and accessories needed to be coordinated carefully. A strong color focus, which included the dark navy and added vibrant peach and turquoise, pulled all of these varied elements together.

The use of pleated shades at the windows was another way of unifying the house, both inside and out. Shade textures varied according to the design treatment of the room. The living and dining room windows had side panels and tiered valances in different patterns, but the same color scheme. The two bedrooms had softly swagged valances and jabots over decorative poles.

Rearranging the furniture in both the ten-by-ten-foot master bedroom and the guest room included placing the beds at an angle in the far corner, thus creating dramatic focal points and increasing the floor space. A peach print and a turquoise solid combined for a theatrical treatment behind the bed in the inviting guest room. The imaginative use of a black Oriental screen as the headboard in Jan and Terrell's master bedroom inspired the introduction of black accents to the peach color.

The tiny kitchen had light wood cabinets and a counter dividing it from the dining room. By adding wallpaper above and below the cabinets, and window shutters with matching fabric, the area took on a fresh, new look. Light stained hardwood floors are enhanced by beautifully patterned area rugs.

Cherished mementos and accessories, like Jan's collection of teacups, are now displayed proudly and enjoyed. Favorite pictures, found hidden away in drawers, have been matted and framed and adorn the once bare walls. Jan was surprised to find that most of her things blended so well with new decorating.

Tennessee interior decorator Mary Ann Weakley helped Jan to explore various ways to handle the home's small spaces. With the decorating successfully completed, Jan admitted that she probably never would have been quite so daring with her colors and furniture arranging, but Mary Ann obviously had listened to her, and knew exactly the feeling she wanted for her home.

Contrary to what one ordinarily hears, the dark and vibrant colors coordinated throughout this house have not only expanded the space visually, but also have set the stage for a home rich with dramatic impact befitting this lovely TV star and her husband.

Chapter 3
Finding Paradise . . .
Master Bedrooms

Our vision of paradise always seems to be of some far-off place. When we imagine a romantic hideaway, it's on the other side of the world, and if we think of a luxurious refuge from the frenzied workplace, we dream of our annual vacation. In reality we could have that intimate, cozy retreat every night of our lives. Finding paradise could be as easy as opening your bedroom door.

At the end of the day, what would be more calming than returning to your own comfortable oasis—a special place that blends your favorite colors and furnishings with your personal things? The master bedroom should be a haven for unwinding and recharging.

The people whose master bedrooms are pictured in this chapter made their dreams come true. They all decided to shower themselves with well-deserved luxury, to give themselves a place to be pampered that would renourish their bodies and souls.

Picture yourself resting on one of these sumptuously covered beds with lots of plump pillows. Imagine quiet times, relaxing and reading on a romantic chaise lounge. Visualize sharing this heavenly place with someone you love. You don't have to wait for your vacation to find a little bit of paradise; it's right there in your own bedroom.

Sunrise . . . Sunset

To wake up every morning in this special room is one of the true joys of my life. Maybe I love it so much because, like a lot of you, I waited so long to decorate it the way I dreamed it should look. Knowing that my husband, Jim, enjoys our bedroom as much as I do has added to my pleasure.

When we become our own clients, decorators suffer the same anxiety as everyone else. If there's anything that makes our situation even more difficult, it's that we have too many choices. We're in the business, so we see new products all the time. When it comes to deciding, we're always in limbo. "Will something better come along?" is our mantra. Sure, something better is bound to come along, but would I want to die in the bedroom in the before picture while I'm waiting?

It's remarkable how everything fell into place once I resolved to move ahead. My love of French country guided the direction of the decorating, and our passion for sunsets over the water was the underlying motivator for the sensual pink and blue color scheme. The magic in the room comes from how well all of our cherished mementos and souvenirs fit into the new design, beginning with a batik ladybug pillow that my stepdaughter, Whitney, made for me one Mother's Day.

A luscious cotton print, spread across the spacious but awkward space, brings the bedroom into focus. The contemporary-style headboard, and the chair and ottoman were reupholstered in the new fabric. Treated to shirring and gathers, the old furniture was made more in keeping with the new softer lines of the room. A ruffled table skirt introduces sea green, and a wool tartan brought back from Scotland combines all of the glorious colors.

Another find is the copper and steel chandelier from Brittany that I had wired and to which I added shades covered in the tartan. Treasured books and accessories fill the custom built-in bookcase, which also houses our TV. The walls are covered with sentimental pictures, my favorite being the Monet adaptation Jim painted.

New Room . . . New Attitude

As a young widow with two teenage sons, Joan Calcaterra felt the need to spruce up her Chicago home. When she began the project, Joan had not counted on the overwhelming change in her attitude toward life. "My fresh new bedroom decor gives me more and more pleasure with each passing day," exclaims the happy owner.

Rebirth of this bedroom began with the choice of fresh soft peach and teal hues. The wall of drapery was replaced by a lush balloon shade gathered on a continental rod. A wallcovering border was used to frame the windows, and the matching pattern covered the once white walls.

A plush peach carpet and the tranquil teal bed treatment continue the softening effect of the room. New mirrored closet doors which replace dark wood ones, visually add space and elegance. Removing a set of doors gives Joan her own private, organized desk area.

Having her sons, Andy and Tom, help her with the prep work saved her money and made it a lot of fun. Now the boys take real pride in their home. "This incredible transformation of my bedroom makes me smile. I feel so different, and every morning when I wake up I feel refreshed," reflects Joan.

Happy Hideaway

$\mathbf{B}$etty and Ed Brooks wanted a change for their master bedroom. They went from dark and drab to light and patterned. The furniture remained the same, but the smashing colors salmon and jade gave their old room a vital new personality. Like most couples they were looking for a design that would be an appealing mixture to please them both.

Balancing bright florals with masculine colors and solid fabrics made it a comfortable retreat for Betty and Ed. When they began remodeling their thirty-nine-year-old ranch house, they decided to turn the master bedroom into more than just a room for sleeping. Betty's addition of a chaise lounge has become her husband's favorite place for reading and watching TV (not seen in photograph; on the wall opposite the bed).

The custom bordered area rug pulls all of the colors together and gives the room its finished look. Since these photographs were taken, Betty has added pictures over the bed and a framed piece of lace adorns the other wall. When the Brookses' two teenage daughters entertain their friends in other parts of the house, Betty and Ed retreat to their own happy hideaway.

New Lifestyle Reflected

A change in the lifestyle of Vermont career woman Rosemary Martell prompted the new look for her outdated master bedroom. After twenty-one years of white French provincial furniture and dark colors, she wanted to create a refreshing new romantic space.

Feminine but not flowery was what Rosemary had in mind. Selecting a soft lilac color for the carpet, so aptly named Ecstasy, was the starting point of her renewal project. Walls were covered in a shimmering paper that made the room glow. A combination of a sophisticated abstract pattern in parfait colors and a solid lilac polished cotton were the perfect companions for the new bedspread and generously padded headboard.

The old windows were replaced with ones that had concealed blinds. Since privacy was not a factor, Rosemary wanted to leave as much of the window exposed as possible. Gently draped lined fabric over a covered rod was the window treatment chosen.

When the room was finished it fulfilled all of Rosemary's decorating desires. She hadn't told anyone that she was redecorating, but on seeing the finished results Rosemary was so excited that she invited her friends to an "Introducing My Bedroom to Society" party.

The flattering muted colors, the feminine but tailored ambience, and the touches of rattan renewed not only the room, but the spirit of its owner. Rosemary told her friends, "I achieved more than I ever dreamed. Now, I truly enjoy being in my bedroom."

For Evergreen

It was a major undertaking, but relocating the master bedroom to the rear of Joy and Joe Butler's home has added immensely to their enjoyment. With the wall between two small rooms removed, the new L-shaped suite provides ample space for the sitting area they always wanted. When a small window was enlarged and a sliding glass door added, the Butlers were able to view, from their bed or lounges, the pool and the canal where they keep their boat.

Joy proclaimed that she didn't like green, but when she made that statement, she wasn't thinking evergreen. When she saw the bold, dark green combined with the cool, grey tile she fell in love with evergreen. Decorating in those two colors, in a mixture of textures, and in finishes from matte to polished, set the stage for glamour. With the king-size bed placed at an angle and facing the mirrored doors that reflect the water view, the drama was heightened.

Streamlined sophistication continues in the double-tiered, padded valance over vertical blinds. Joy used fabric to cover a pedestal and added the three-panel screen, in a square pattern repeating the floor design, to accent a corner. The room's vertical and horizontal lines were relieved by the sinuous curves of the bench at the foot of the bed and rounded backs of Joe's chair and Joy's chaise.

The reaction of friends who see the spectacular suite is an admiring sigh. But, more important is the Butlers' joy as they relax in their soothing suite enjoying the new environment and the great view.

Sweet Slumber

When a couple from up north decided to move to a warmer climate, they began by shedding the trappings of big city living. The dark colors and the heavy mahogany furniture were left behind. Moving into a one-level townhouse villa gave them less indoor space to take care of, and extra time to enjoy a more leisurely lifestyle.

Setting the color palette for the master bedroom is a soothing seafoam green plush carpet, and surrounding the room is an abstact wallcovering in pastel greens and pinks. Fabrics in the same soft color vein enhance a reproduction white and brass Victorian bed. White wicker and pine furniture continue the lighter look, while a skirted vanity and bench are a charming, yet practical addition.

Brass swing arm wall lamps free up table space and adjust for the proper lighting. The choice of accessories and furnishings gives this contemporary home a classic romantic feeling. What northern couple would not enjoy moving into this sunny Florida bedroom?

Pulling It All Together

New

Wall-to-wall carpet

Wallcovering

Furniture

Window treatment

Bed ensemble

Swing arm lamps

Our Blue Heaven

Pulling It All Together

Old

Carpet

New

Window treatment

Headboard, comforter, dust
    ruffle, and pillows

Skirted tables

Bench

Chaise lounge

For a busy professional couple, having a luxurious bedroom to retire to at the end of the day has to be a number one priority. Several years ago, Beth and Lee Marquardt moved into an older house in Dallas, Texas. Initially they were busy with general fixing-up projects, but eventually they decided to create a master bedroom haven.

The only thing the Marquardts decided they could live with was the light mauve tinted carpet. The decorating scheme began to evolve when Beth found the sophisticated country florals and ribbon stripe, all in deep, rich colors. Beginning with the generous draperies and top treatment, the windows took on new proportions and added elegance.

A padded headboard, richly gathered dust ruffle, outline quilted comforter demurely tied at the corners, and a multitude of pillows mixing patterns and solids create a heavenly setting for bedtime. With a comfortable chaise lounge for reading, a padded bench for pure beauty, and skirted tables to hold lamps and cherished pictures, Beth and Lee have the romantic room about which they always dreamed.

Pink Panache

It was Pat Dellorfano's idea to introduce luscious pinks to brighten up her spacious master bedroom. Decorated sixteen years ago in the then-fashionable earth tones, the room needed a complete color change. Her husband, Fred, was concerned about using pastels, but ended up loving the romantic new look.

A glorious floral chintz in spring garden colors was chosen as the main pattern for the room. The outline quilted scalloped coverlet and dust ruffle, throw pillow, and the refreshing window treatment are all fabricated out of the chintz. A table is gracefully skirted in a pastel silk plaid.

The Dellorfanos' French-style furniture was recovered in a deep rosy pink flamestitch textured fabric. Two benches at the foot of the bed were updated in soft celadon green, and their unusual shellback chair has a new mini-patterned fabric on an ecru background.

Rearranging the furniture has opened up the room, and now Pat and Fred can take advantage of the natural light in their sunny reading and conversational area. The folding mirrored screen makes a luxurious corner backdrop, doubling the impact of the new decorating scheme.

Keeping all their furniture and accessories, but changing to new and vibrant colors, has given new life to this lovely room and to the people who live in it.

Suite Dreams

Pulling It All Together

Old
Furniture
Shutters

New
Window treatments
Wall paint
Bed treatment
Bench recovered

The first time Gay Morris saw this large master bedroom with its ten-foot ceilings, she knew it would be perfect to show off her grand-scale mahogany furniture. But after moving into her North Carolina ranch house, she found the taste of the previous owner not to her liking. The room felt cavernous and cold. Gay knew that she and her husband Kent would not be happy for long in this predominantly white bedroom.

Another problem presented itself. Even though the shuttered windows offered complete privacy, they did not totally block out the light on this sunny side of the house. A treatment was designed that took advantage of the built-in crown moulding cornice. By adding drapery panels and a softly gathered valance that covered the two-foot space from the top of the window to the ceiling, the window became an important feature of the room. Now all Gay has to do is release the tiebacks, and the drapery with its blackout lining gives her complete darkness.

Painting the walls a deep, rich plum—computer matched to the dust ruffle fabric color—creates the warm environment that the Morrises were looking for. The grand proportions of the king-sized four-poster bed are brought into scale by introducing a traditional floral outline quilted coverlet in soft, muted colors contrasted with the dark plum ruffle.

A finishing touch to this classically elegant room is the graceful Chippendale bench recovered in a serene cotton strie. From now on it's sweet dreams for the Morrises in their plum perfect bedroom.

Country Chic

This lovely home is the dream creation of Phyllis and Rob Myers. Two years ago, Rob built this classic Southern home with two gracious front porches. But when it came to decorating the interior he turned the house over to Phyllis. Working with things they already had, she gave the rooms warmth and sparkle.

Creating a chic country bedroom entailed not only selecting the lush fabrics and color scheme, but doing some of the labor herself. Rather than leaving the walls painted a flat color, Phyllis had them painted gray, and then she feather-dusted the pink of the ceiling over all of the walls. The effect makes the room glow.

Contrasted with the subtle pink, Phyllis chose dramatic black, giving the room a comfortable, yet sophisticated look. Pale flower blossoms strewn over black ground is the pattern fabric used at the window for balloon valances, for a table throw, and for the bed. The bed ensemble is completed with a pink and white swag print, which is also seen on the settee's cushions and pillows.

More of Phyllis' handiwork can be seen in the clever way she spruced up her old lampshades (using the plastic covers that come with the shades as her pattern) in the same black moiré fabric as the tableskirt. She found the wicker settee at a garage sale and painted it black.

Beginning with only the handsome brass bed, Phyllis has managed—with her very personal touches—to bring life and love to their bedroom.

New Closets and Colors
Completely Change Bedroom

Pulling It All Together

Old

Furniture

New

Built-in closets

Furniture arrangement

Wallpaper and border

Window treatment

Bed ensemble

As often happens when people are "in the business," their own homes are usually the last places to be decorated. Interior decorator Carol Stearns and her husband Al's master bedroom was one of those places. After ten years of living in the same home, they had completely outgrown their eleven-by-fifteen-foot master bedroom. The Stearnses had no desire to move, so they decided to remodel instead.

The room's one small closet provided very limited storage space. Carol's answer was to construct two closets and overhead storage, which when finished, created a niche for their queen-size bed. As a result, because the closets take up the area of two end tables, no floor space was eliminated. Now, wall pockets provide a place for bedtime books and essentials. When needed, clip-on lights are attached to the bedpost. The project tripled the closet space and enabled the Stearnses to store little-used items out of the way over the bed. Using the same furniture, a more interesting arrangement was achieved with the bed as the focal point.

Teal and peach make up the room's lush color scheme in coordinating fabric patterns. A matching wallpaper border accents the bed and the ceiling line. The window treatment combines a continental rod pocketed, tapered valance in the striped fabric with peach mini-blinds. A quilted bedspread, striped dust ruffle, and matching pillow shams complete the bed ensemble.

Two dachshunds are the inspiration for the Stearnses' collection of dog artifacts, which they now have room to display and enjoy. What once was an outdated, disorganized, and cluttered room has become a fashionable, composed, and restful master bedroom retreat.

Paisley Perfect Compromise

When Jeanette and Kent Young moved into a larger home in Oklahoma, they found they could live with the house as it was, except for the master bedroom. It was a spacious room with windows that overlooked old trees—and in particular, a nest of birds—but the interior view was not quite so appealing.

The Youngs needed to come up with a solution to a typical challenge. Jeanette wanted their bedroom to be frothy and feminine, but Kent found this look not to his liking. They both agreed that the uneven line of the chair rail and window sill was visually disturbing, and a solution needed to be found.

Following the color direction—deep mauves and blue—set by the rest of the house, a paisley in these rich colors was the perfect compromise, feminine but not fussy. The tailored drapery treatment left the scenery in view, covered the uneven trim problem, and framed the windows in the paisley fabric. A window heading combining a brass rod over two continental rods carries out the refined look of the room.

Their comfortable chair and ottoman were recovered in a coordinating fabric, and a multi stripe was used to cover two occasional chairs and for accent pillows. Wallcovering in a mini-paisley pattern was installed below the chair rail.

A pleasant surprise was how well the Youngs' collection of Doel Reed aquatints fit in with their new quietly elegant master bedroom.

Stunning Suite

Making this master bedroom suite into a stunning area with great visual impact was the owners' desire. Selecting a dramatic black and sand color scheme with accents of turquoise and metallic gold set the tone of this grand suite.

Dramatic contrast was achieved with a high-style contemporary fabric that was used for the bed comforter and the softly draped window swag. The tailored dust ruffle, tableskirt, and an armless upholstered chair were covered in a black cotton solid and a mini-print. Turquoise accents were picked up in the lamp base, swag lining, and throw pillows.

This sophisticated direction was also carried into the master bathroom, creating a total look for a splendid suite.

Pulling It All Together

New

Patterned fabric

    Window swag

    Comforter

Black fabrics

    Dust ruffle

    Tableskirt

    Chair

Accessories

A Texas-Size Miracle

Joan Rudloff, the founder of Heart & Home, a country-style accessory business, was making arrangements for a meeting of her representatives. While she was firming up the hotel plans with the banquet manager, she said that she wished the plans for decorating her Texas house were going as well. Joan explained that she was giving a reception at her home in two weeks for the visiting representatives, but because her husband had been ill she had not gotten around to decorating.

The hotel manager suggested that she get in touch with his wife, Necole, who had her own interior decorating business. He felt confident that Necole could help her. Joan responded, "I don't think you realize how bad a condition my house is in. It would take a miracle to decorate it before the party!"

Skeptical, but willing at least to talk to Necole Querbach, a weary Joan had her come by the next evening. For three hours Necole interviewed Joan, finding out everything she could about her client-to-be. The next evening Necole returned with a plan. She first presented her color scheme, fabric, wallcovering, paint, and carpet selections. Then she explained that she had all of the products and subcontractors lined up. All she needed was Joan's okay to proceed, and she would guarantee that the job would be completed in twelve days. The next morning everything was set in motion, and in twelve days the transformation was completed.

One of the rooms decorated was the Rudloffs' master bedroom. Necole carried the Victorian garden theme into the room, introducing teals to a pink palette. An unusual border treatment was carried around the walls of the room. The crisp floral print in soft blues and greens is used to dress the windows and the exquisite antique brass bed.

Having the bedroom finished for the party met an urgent priority, but having a relaxing and refreshing retreat for Joan and her husband to come home to fulfilled a daily need. It is no small miracle to have created so much pleasure in someone's life.

Chapter 4
Lovely Living Rooms

Once upon a time living rooms were decorated, then reserved for company only. But, despite their intended purpose, these formidable-looking rooms did nothing to welcome guests. Instead, everybody retreated to the family room, where they could feel comfortable, and the living room remained empty.

An even worse scenario is the furniture-empty living room. People buy a home and then put off decorating the living room. Rather than settle for something less than their ultimate dream room, the new homeowners wait—sometimes for years—to furnish their living room. In the meantime they have to pass a barren room every day.

The appeal of the living rooms shown in this chapter is that they are lived in. However beautiful and finished they appear, these rooms are used daily, not saved for company only. The unique decorating style of each room reflects the individual taste and personality of the owners.

A gracious living room should be one that welcomes all, but most especially you. After all, shouldn't this be the place where you are living now, and happily ever after?

Mum's the Word

When it was time to update the mood of Marian Welch's living room, this North Carolinian knew that she wanted a lighter, more elegant look—something more in keeping with the beautiful Oriental pieces she and her husband had collected while traveling all over the world. A decorating theme was devised around two things she didn't want to change, the rust wall-to-wall carpeting and a favorite armchair.

An Oriental-inspired print, appropriately named Kasumi, a subtle mum pattern, in shades of pewter and parchment with cinnamon—the newer version of rust—was used at the window. The generously swagged valance and jabots frame the soft-colored pleated shades. Two tuxedo arm loveseats replace the old armless ones, and their new arrangement allows for a more spacious-looking room.

It also shows off the custom mum design of the new area rug. Laid over the old carpet, the rug lightens up the once dark floor. Parsons end tables in black lacquer blend well with the Oriental mood of the room. Brighter colors and more formal furnishings, carefully rearranged, give this living room a refined elegance befitting the lady who lives there.

Victorian Miracle Continued

ontinuing the story of Necole Querbach's decorating the Rudloffs' home in twelve days is this lovely Victorian living room. Necole picked the vibrant colors to set the tone of her garden scheme from Joan Rudloff's American beauty rose china that she had inherited from her mother.

Wanting a real change from the old earth tones, they began by painting the dark paneling, and even the upright piano, bright white. A dusty rose carpet and a glorious floral fabric in redrose, pink, and plant green gave this Victorian living room a fresh new look. All the charming accessories from Joan's Heart & Home country craft business, and the classic 1928 Wurlitzer jukebox, had finally found the proper setting.

In the beginning Joan doubted that this room would come together in the extraordinarily short time she had. When the decorating was completed, she was more overwhelmed by the beauty of her gorgeous new living room than by the absolute miracle of having met her deadline.

Pulling It All Together

New

Interior restoration

Paint colors

Fabrics; large floral, mini
    print, small pattern, and
    solid
        Upholstered furniture
        Window treatment
        Table skirt
        Pillows

Tables

Area rug

Eclectic Elegance in a Small Space

The eclectic taste of a young couple, Angela and Leonard Mindlin, was the springboard for turning their first house, a typical ranch, into a charming and sophisticated home. They began by replacing three plain, narrow windows with one large, mullioned picture window. Besides adding more light, the new window created an impressive focal point for the living room.

The pale yellow tint of the luxurious brocade sofas and chairs is repeated softly throughout the room. A large Oriental rug in pale blue, rose, and apricot introduces new colors to the elegant palette. Framing the window is an elaborately swagged, bowed, and puddled treatment in a shimmering silk plaid.

Bleached pine Louis XV-style tables continue the bright, airy look. Rather than using a solid wood coffee table, the glass top reflects light and opens up a view to the rug's center medallion. Fulfilling one of Angela's wishes is a white baby grand piano romantically angled in the corner.

The soft colors, appropriately scaled furniture so artfully arranged, and personal style of the Mindlins gives a small living room a spacious and inviting ambience. Their eclectic selection of accessories adds character and the finishing touch to this luxurious living room.

Pulling It All Together

New

Window

Swagged drapery treatment

Furniture

Area rug

Baby grand piano

Bright Floral Fabric Lifts Family Spirits

In preparation for the return of her children for the Christmas holidays, Alice Newsome, the recently widowed owner of this gracious North Carolina home built in the early 1900s, wanted to update and brighten her living room. It had been twenty-five years since the house had last been decorated. Alice's idea was to give this room a cheery and inviting feeling, but she wanted to achieve it with a minimum amount of disruption. She wanted to keep her existing furniture and not recover the cherry red sofa. She also didn't want to repaint the avocado green moldings and trim.

Introducing a bright, but soft, floral pattern fabric in shades of reds, pinks, leafy greens, with a touch of cornflower blue, produced an extraordinary transformation to the once subdued room. This charming cotton fabric was used to recover two comfortable wood-framed chairs, for pillows that updated the red sofa, and for the softly swagged drapery treatment. White mini-blinds completed the new look at the window.

An ottoman from another room and a chair were greatly enhanced by being recovered in a small rose-colored print. The addition of ruffles softens the hard lines of these two pieces of furniture. An existing dark rug was replaced with an Oriental that incorporated the new color scheme on a rich navy background.

Alice's cherishables, like her grandmother's shadow box, took on a whole different meaning in their bright, new surroundings. When her family returned home for the holidays, all of their favorite things were still in place, but their spirits were lifted at the sight of the new look, which managed to bring the old and updated together in beautiful harmony.

Rich Raspberry Warms Up All-White Living Room

The owners of this spacious home felt the need to warm up their living room. Used primarily for entertaining family and friends, the all-white room appeared forbidding and uninviting.

"We'll replace the wall-to-wall carpet with hardwood floors, but we want to keep all of our furniture," was their plan. The eclectic collection of French, Oriental, and contemporary furnishings needed to be pulled together to provide a striking, but comfortable feeling.

Introduction of a rich raspberry and accents of teal was the starting point of the transformation. The sofa and sectionals remained white, but a paisley pattern in the new colors was used to recover two French pickled wood-frame chairs. White sheers at the window were replaced by tailored balloon shades in a sumptuous teal fabric, and overlayered with pinch-pleated draw draperies in the raspberry and teal paisley. Colorful throw pillows softened the white sofa.

The sophisticated calla lily pattern of the custom area rug brought together all of the colors of the room. The owners' collection of fine Oriental art and objects, grand French armoire, and personal accessories were given a new life in their new warm, colorful home.

Southwestern Style

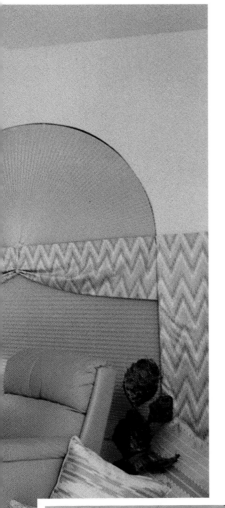

Thisc house began its life as a builder's model, but it quickly became home to a couple who had retired to Florida. They couldn't help but be attracted to the soothing atmosphere of the serene southwestern interior decorating.

Steering away from the more vibrant colors usually associated with this look, Carole Ponzio decided to decorate in more muted desert colors. She let the deep greens of the cactus and other plants provide color contrast, as well as the rich color and texture of the rough-sawn cedar fireplace.

A classic dhurrie rug warms up the white vinyl floor and anchors the furniture arrangement. Pleated shades at the windows softly accent the arches. The textured sheer shades are framed by a cotton fabric with a flamestitch pattern.

The pine entertainment center houses the TV and VCR. Cube end tables and a large coffee table resemble marble, but are laminated. The recessed brass bases of the tables pick up on the diagonal brass strip of the fireplace.

Faux stone lamps and vases complete the southwestern feeling of this earthy room that was really decorated to be lived in.

Pulling It All Together

New

Furniture

Area rug

Window treatments

Lamps

One Pattern . . . Three Different Colors

Pulling It All Together

Old

Neutral wallcovering

Neutral vertical blinds

White Haitian cotton
    sectional sofa

Natural wicker furniture

New

Add one print fabric in three
    colorways
        Window cornice
        Round tableskirt
        Extra large pillows

Paint wicker furniture black

Rearranged sectional sofa

A fashionable young Illinois wife and mother, Jeanetta Sutherland, wanted a more dramatic look for her living room. After installing a textured wallcovering with a warm, neutral background, a white Haitian cotton sectional sofa, and vinyl pinstriped vertical blinds, she felt the room was too bland.

Jeanetta and her husband, Randy, love black, so she was delighted when she found a contemporary floral in mauve on a black background. She then cleverly brought in two other fabrics in the same pattern, but in two different color schemes. The result was a living room without the blahs.

A simple treatment of a cornice was installed over the vertical blinds enhancing the overall look of the window. The teal fabric was used for extra large throw pillows and a skirted table. Jeanetta painted wicker accent tables and an etagere black. Rearranging the sectional sofa opened the room up and made it look more spacious.

With the daring use of color and prints, and a little of her own labor, Jeanetta was able to convert this once plain living room into an exciting oasis.

Restored Living Room Becomes a Very Special Place

With their own hands, a young career couple with two children have lovingly restored this ninety-four-year-old New Jersey farmhouse. Redoing their home on weekends became Judy and Jim Knox's hobby. Together they plastered and painted, replaced the windows, uncovered pocket doors, and recreated mouldings.

They were delighted when they saw the gracious floral fabric in wine red and cornflower blue on an ivory background because it was exactly what they had in mind. Walls were painted a daring dark winterberry color, and the mouldings and trim a clear oyster white.

The Knoxes' old living room furniture was moved to the family room, clearing the way to create the traditional English feeling they desired. Two comfortable wingback chairs in a blue mini-print, and a camelback sofa in the charming floral, brought the glorious new colors into the room. An additional small-patterned fabric was used to skirt a table. A glass and brass coffee table over a bordered rug made a lovely accent area, while matching Queen Anne cherry end tables complete the new furniture.

The elegant lined floral swag and jabot installed under the restored moulding allows lots of natural light into the room. This bright and inviting room has now become Judy and Jim's very special place.

Luxurious Living

Long before Gary and Cecilia Peters moved into their home in Florida, they had been collectors of western art. They were particularly fond of the authentic art of the Sioux and Zumi Indians. The Peterses' splendid living room has been decorated to set off their favorite pieces.

Lavish leather sectional sofas and chairs are arranged to take advantage of the panoramic landscape, both exterior and interior. The impressive expanse of window is covered with soft sheers, but cornices and draperies in a dark-patterned fabric frame the windows. Mixing textures, and combining tailored elements with more graceful lines, contributes to the pleasing feeling of the room.

The Peterses' warm colors, personal artifacts, and graceful window treatments add drama and excitement to this comfortably luxurious living room.

Comfortable Contemporary

A beautiful new brick and stone ranch house with a river view is now the dream home of Wilburn and Virginia Sutherland of St. Charles, Illinois. They have always preferred neutral colors and textures to create what Virginia calls a "comfortable contemporary" look. In decorating their new home they kept to the subtle tones, but added new sparkle when they introduced brass accents and touches of blue.

Virginia chose a silky textured fabric in a southwestern pattern for the two loveseats, then repeated the fabric in the window cornice. The vertical blinds allow them regulation of light, privacy, and the river view. Never having used wallpaper before, the Sutherlands were pleasantly surprised by its elegant look and easy maintenance.

Lines were kept straight except for the round glass and brass coffee table that matches the brass etageres. The rich beige area rug has a decorative blue border, and pillows and the cornice as well are also treated to blue welting and banding.

The Sutherlands were content with their lifestyle, and never desired any drastic redecorating. The subtle changes, keeping with warm neutrals and adding a measure of cool blue, gave them a newer, more formal look, without intruding on the established Sutherland "comfortable contemporary" feeling.

Historic Maryland Home

William Chesley, the owner of this historic Prince George's County, Maryland, home wanted to make the interior more compatible with its 1790 facade. One of his major concerns was changing the color emphasis from dark earth tones to a lighter and more elegant color palette. The other was devising a scheme that would allow him to keep the existing window treatments.

The major decorating project began with selecting lighter hues from the stripe and floral pattern of the drapery fabric for the new color scheme of salmon, aqua, and ivory. An exquisite striped brocade combining these hues was chosen for the traditional loveseats. Beautiful hardwood floors were uncovered when the rust wall-to-wall carpet was removed. A custom area rug with a flowered, banded border enhanced the newly mellow stained floors.

Formal mahogany Queen Anne furniture replaced the existing contemporary furnishings. The unique arrangement of the loveseats back to back in the center of the room made the room more suitable for entertaining small groups. Painting the walls a pale salmon created a warm glow that suits the elegant new look. Oriental art, bowls, and figurines complete the interior decorating.

Once again this beautifully proportioned living room, with its twelve-foot ceilings, has the gracious ambience it deserves.

Decorator Creates
Her Own Dream Room

After years of living in a traditional style home in the Washington, D.C., area, Peggy Walsh and her husband relocated to Tampa, Florida. The warmer climate and the more informal feeling of their new stucco home prompted the Walshes to think about changing their decorating direction.

The charm of their house was its open floor plan, with one room flowing into the other. Peggy felt that the formal arrangement of her traditional furniture didn't suit the house. Even though she was a professional interior decorator, she was faced with the same challenges every redecorating project holds . . . where to start, how much to spend, and what colors and materials to choose from the overwhelming array available.

The Walshes lived with their existing furnishings for several years before they decided to revamp their living room totally. Changing the carpet was the starting point. Using plum and teal, the Walshes designed a graceful serpentine pattern for the carpet. An elegant marbled fabric, in shades of the new colors with gold metallic accents, was the perfect choice for the new curved sectional sofa and softly swagged window treatment.

The drapery fabric was lined in a plum cotton that was also used on the chair. New glass-top tables with black lacquer bases added an elegant touch and worked exceptionally well with the Walshes' new baby grand piano. The only pieces the Walshes kept from their old possessions were the green lamps which worked so well in the new environment.

It is always most difficult for an interior decorator to do her own home, but Peggy met her challenge by designing an elegant, but contemporary ambience that matches her Florida lifestyle.

Updated Traditional Living Room

T ired of the predominently white and gold living room in their twenty-year-old Massachusetts house, Beverly and Raymond Tarr decided to update their colors and decorating scheme. Keeping a very large grand piano and a traditional feeling were to be part of the master plan.

A rich mauve and blue cabbage rose print was selected for the new sofa and the tailored window treatments. Full drapery panels were hung under a matching cornice board for window framing treatments. Off-white sheers provide privacy while allowing natural light to filter into the room. A pair of Queen Anne wingback chairs, in a luxurious mauve stripe, have become the ideal setting for the Tarrs' favorite pastime of reading.

The richly textured string wallcovering ties the colors together and provides an interesting contrast to the taupe carpet. Beverly painted the wall behind the bookcases a mellow mauve, and added finishing touches with traditional occasional tables and accessories.

Working with a master plan and a timetable provided the Tarrs with a realistic guide to achieving their goal of a fashionable new living room in four months.

Relaxed View

Moving to Florida brings a change of view, both literally and figuratively, to the new owners of this gracious townhouse. They were ready for warmer climes, but not quite ready to retire or depart completely from their previous formal style of living and entertaining.

The living room/dining room combination is set for their new southern hospitality. By creating a serenely elegant decorating style and color scheme this couple was ready not only for guests, but for a refreshing private lifestyle as well. Seafoam green pulls the restful colors of the Florida landscape into the room. Combining abstract patterns with solids, and adding pink to the aquas, greens, and crisp white, gives the house a light and airy feeling.

A shimmering stretch of draped fabric over covered poles accents the window without distracting from the view. Furnishings are eclectic, from a Louis XV armchair to a contemporary glass-top pedestal dining table. The openness of both these pieces makes them ideal for smaller spaces.

The relaxing view from their windows belies the active lifestyle of these very active northern transplants.

So Nice to Come Home To

After years of moving with the Air Force, Maria and Tom Connell have finally settled in Fort Walton Beach, Florida. The Connells feel lucky to have found this spacious home where they can surround themselves with all the lovely collectables they have gathered from their travels in the United States and abroad.

The uncomplicated lines of their contemporary home are repeated in the clean, crisp feeling of the decorating. Picking up on the pink tint of the fireplace stone, a soft sheer with just a tint of pink was selected for the large expanse of windows. To complement the Connells' brass accessories, brass rods were chosen to hang the draperies.

A luxuriously pillowed white sofa and two cherry Oriental chairs with rose brocade cushions create a comfortable seating arrangement around the fireplace. The serene striped wallpaper adds a nice touch to the built-in bookcase.

"What a pleasure to be nestled in this tranquil environment. It's the first time I feel we could be happy in one place forever," Maria contentedly exclaims.

Chapter 5
The Pleasures of Dining

Dining conjures up a variety of images . . . intimate dinners with a spouse . . . evening meals with the children . . . family get-togethers for holidays and special occasions . . . and entertaining friends.

The dream rooms on the following pages are decorated to enhance and prolong the pleasures of dining. Each of the rooms makes a very personal statement about the lifestyle of the owner. The design direction and color scheme are in keeping with the rest of the home, and provide the perfect setting to display and enjoy cherished china, silver, and crystal.

Delicious colors, tempting patterns, and luscious accessories promise relaxation and stimulate conversation. Many of the most memorable events of one's life can be traced to leisurely times spent around the dining table.

Joie de Vivre

For twelve years the Waterses looked for just the right pieces of furniture for their dining room. Then, while antiquing in her Texas hometown one day, Nancy Waters was able to put an end to her search. A Francophile at heart, Nancy's dream of creating an elegant French room began to take shape.

The handsome ca. 1905 walnut furniture with inlaid detailing included chairs with their original red velvet upholstery. To complement this magnificent find, Nancy wanted a glamorous window treatment. A rich Parisian feeling was created using a romantic old gold moiré swag and bustle window appointment with ivory and rouge flourishes. Graceful bordered lace covers the window.

A moiré table runner accenting the Waterses' collection of vermeil flatware, and their exquisite china and crystal set a grand table for entertaining in the French manner. Never slaves to trends, the Waterses have their own sense of style and their own *joie de vivre,* joy in living.

On a Grand Scale

The twenty-five-foot ceiling of this dramatic dining room demanded decoration on a grand scale. Cecilia and Gary Peters, the owners of this fabulous home, have managed to take an imposing structure and inject it with warmth and comfort.

While antiquing the Peterses came across a set of furniture made in America at the turn of the century. Their keen decorating sense told them that the scale and proportions of the furniture would be perfect for their dining room. Now the heavily carved china cabinet, table, and ten chairs grace their imposing room.

For the stately windows Cecilia and Gary wanted a treatment that would enhance their height without being too light and airy, or too dark and heavy. A nice compromise was achieved with the patterned, tapered balloon valances and the sheer draperies. Gathered sheers in the arches added the finishing touch.

Majestic proportions tempered with rich wood, comfortable upholstery, and billowing window treatments make dining with the Peterses a grand affair.

One of a Kind

Looking to further dramatize the recessed ceiling of the dining room in this Michigan home, Mary Bahar designed an exotic tented ceiling. Created out of an inexpensive peach-colored sheer, the awesome effect far exceeded the cost. A lush green wall continues the unique decorating theme.

The selection of a paisley fabric in green with swirls of magenta and peach for the window treatment and the fully upholstered chairs complements the spirit of the room. A sand-colored rug further echos the exotic desert ambience.

The brass and glass dining table, chandelier, and accessories help to unify the elements in the room. Mary's stunning decorating conveys the appealing combination of elegance and comfort.

A Passion for 18th-Century English

Even though Paula and Ray Uhlirs' Virginia townhome was on a smaller scale than the stately houses Paula had admired in England, she did not let that stop her from adapting the look to their new residence. Instead, Paula let her passion for 18th-century furnishings determine the decorating direction.

It might have been too bold for some people, but when Paula found the rich Chinese red wallcovering she knew it was right for her dining room. The Oriental pattern is based on a design from London's Victoria and Albert Museum collection. The color and pattern are repeated in the refined swag and cascades that enhance the window without overpowering the room. Painting the trim and wainscoting white also visually increased the small room's proportions.

The addition of a ceiling rosette gave importance to the chandelier. Scaled-down accent furniture displays Paula's English teacup collection and porcelains. All these elements serve as an elegant background for the handsome Chippendale dining table and chairs.

If you really desire a particular look, don't be afraid to adapt it to the space you have. Paula proved that it can be done, and it doesn't have to cost a fortune either. That's one nice thing about small spaces; they take a lot less of everything.

Country Collections

This charming country dining room is deceiving. Even though it is colonial in feeling, everyone is surprised to find out that this Rockport, Massachusetts, house was built only six years ago. The Tebos wanted the proper setting for their varied collections of country antiques.

Eileen Tebo's doll collection inspired the unusual window treatment. After she found the cornice boards that depict scenes of folk and rag dolls, Eileen created a window treatment that would enhance the cornices.

Two coordinating patterns, a mini-print and a floral stripe, were chosen in delicate mauve, green, and blue on a light beige background. The mini-print was used for the cafe curtain that is installed on a spring tension rod. To see more of the view of the rock garden, the curtains have a center opening. In addition, the rod can be removed easily.

The new crossbeam was hand-hewn by a Rockport craftsman. The other beams have been left in their natural state, as has the tongue and groove ceiling. The Tebos' vast basket collection is hung from the rafters. Their lovely collection of antique oak furniture is well suited to the new room.

A coordinating wallpaper in the floral stripe pattern covers the walls, and the mini-print fabric has been used to line the old icebox that was given a modern-day use. A one-of-a-kind stained glass rose and blue light fixture was custom-made by a friend.

These avid collectors, with their found treasures and the cherished pieces custom-made for them by their craftsmen friends, bring continuing joy to all those who share their comfortable dining room.

In the Oriental Mood

In decorating their dining room, Maria and Tom Connell continued the soft tones and Oriental inspiration of their living room. A black lacquer Chinese screen adds dramatic contrast and vitality to this soothing soft pink room.

Two odd-shaped windows were unified with cornices installed to give the windows the appearance of the same height and depth. Privacy was not a factor, so slightly textured sheer draperies complete the window treatment. A wallpaper border in the same subtle colors, and with curved lines similar to the cornice, emphasizes the refined, elegant feeling of the room.

The handsome table and chairs reflect traditional chippendale lines. Many pleasant hours are passed in the Connells' tranquil dining room.

Chapter 6
Send in the Cooks . . . Kitchens

Besides being practical places for preparing sustenance for the body, kitchens should be beautiful spaces that provide nourishment to the soul. Efficient workspace and storage is the starting point to a well-planned kitchen. But just as important as functional design, is a decorating scheme that conveys a pleasant and cheerful mood.

Customizing your kitchen can mean starting from scratch, where all of your options are open. More often though, it's updating what you already have. Perhaps it's time to replace the flooring with a newer, easier to care for vinyl in a lighter color. Dingy-looking cabinets could be refinished or painted, and countertops covered with a new laminate or ceramic tile to add fresh sparkle.

The most effective way to add color and pattern, and set the decorating direction of a kitchen, is with wallcovering. Carrying the paper above the cabinets and into the breakfast area, and perhaps adding a border, will breathe life into the room. Complete the look by adding coordinating fabric at the windows, and in the eating area with placemats and seat cushions, or a luxuriously full tableskirt. What a bright and stylish way to greet the day!

Perfect Collaboration

Though divided by a counter and different flooring, the remodeled kitchen and new breakfast room addition come together as one great room in this house. When Debbie and Roy MacDonald bought their 1924 suburban Atlanta, Georgia home, they began a major renovation project starting with the totally revamped kitchen space. Although they personally did 60 percent of the work, they enlisted local talent to give it a very special handcrafted look.

After the kitchen was totally gutted, new cabinets in a nutmeg stain and white countertops were installed. An artisan specially grinded the colors for the hand-painted tiles above the counter to match perfectly the exquisitely colored floral wallcovering in the adjoining area. Another Atlanta artist created the stained glass panels for the cabinet doors.

Mexican variegated floor tiles were painstakingly laid by the MacDonalds. Interior decorator, Terry Clemons, suggested the deep rose color for the far wall, which is repeated as a ceiling border in the kitchen. A braided rug woven in coordinating colors makes a handsome addition to the hardwood floor.

Simple shutters enhance the graceful arched windows. The MacDonalds' wonderful country antiques fit in perfectly with the new informal style of decorating. Wall shelves hold Debbie's collection of old blue and white Delft, which she's mixed with her newer china and ceramic pieces.

The end result, from the MacDonalds' hands-on labor to the collaboration of many talented people, is a perfectly lovely area in which to enjoy family cooking and dining.

Nantucket Natural

A small house was built recently on Nantucket for Pat and Fred Dellorfano and their five children. They wanted the decorating of this summer cottage to be totally different from their Boston residence. They have managed to turn this new house into a small gem.

In the Dellorfanos' large eat-in kitchen, simple treatments to complement their pine antique reproduction furniture were what this room called for. The country patterns used in the wallcovering and fabric are in colors of navy and periwinkle blue with accents of green and cherry red. Bay windows have pleated shades for use when privacy is required, topped with a sharp navy print valance gathered on a rod.

The matching fabric is used on seatpads for the dining chairs. Three wallpaper patterns have been cleverly coordinated, a large block plaid, a cherry print border, and a sponge-patterned paper.

The natural and gracious feeling of Nantucket has been retained in the decorating direction of this charming family-centered room.

Clean-Lined Country

The common perception of country conjurs up a busy, and in some instances, overdone decorating style. As with most things, it's all in the interperation. When Lynn and Bob Ardizzone dreamt of having a country kitchen, they invisioned a crisp blue and white color scheme, clean lines, and a total lack of clutter.

After they inherited a seventy-year-old home, the Ardizzones decided to start from scratch and design a plan for a new kitchen. Following their dream, they began by selecting white painted wood cabinets and a clear, bright French blue for the countertops. The square pattern of the white tile splashboard is repeated in the new flooring.

A Matisse-like design covers the walls in the breakfast area. Matching fabric is seen in the tablecloth and window treatments that go country with blue ruffles. Across the ceiling of the entire room is a wallpaper border, and a coordinating mini-paper is used on the remaining walls. The graceful lines of the honey-stained French chairs give the room variety in color and style.

Without resorting to overdone cute and clutter, Lynn and Bob have achieved the rare and crisp country kitchen they envisioned.

French Country on the Cape

Looks can be deceiving, but you can find this charming kitchen in a new Cape Cod home. Having a taste for French country food and homes, interior decorator Linda Risley designed her new kitchen in the manner of Provence.

In travels with her husband, Dan, she has collected seventy-five pieces of copper from all over Europe and the Middle East. Now Linda can provide the ideal setting to display her intriguing finds. Look closely and you can see more of her copper reflected in the window.

The Risleys' handsome antique German stoneware was the inspiration for the kitchen's cool colors. White walls and countertops contrast with the dark wood tones of the cabinets, while soft blue treatments dress up the windows.

But when it came to designing the kitchen, Linda did more than is usually expected of an interior decorator. She and her husband carried out all of the finish work, including tiling the countertops and the floor. It took four months, but now Linda and Dan have their French Provincial kitchen on the Cape.

Major Remodeling

A remarkable transformation was achieved in the nine-year-old Michigan house of interior decorator Judy Roessler, and husband Walter, after she decided to tackle her own kitchen. The existing space no longer served the day-to-day needs of a family of four.

Judy made two major changes—she removed the divider wall that separated the family room and moved the wall on the right back several feet. These changes opened up the floor plan of the kitchen and gave her more storage and working space. New light pecan finished cabinets and white countertops visually brighten the room.

The half-round window over the sink adds natural light, and a combination of ceiling fixtures spreads light throughout the room. A subdued blue on white color scheme is combined on the floor, in two reverse matching wallpapers and a ceiling border, and in the country check of the tablecloth.

Carpet and cabinets were angled to make the transition from kitchen to family room. The fanback Windsor chairs and pedestal table and the Roesslers' canister collection took on a new look in their revamped modern environment.

Almond Delight

For the city couple moving to a new townhouse this dreamy, spacious kitchen was a welcome sight. Pale colors and luxurious details were combined in this well laid out kitchen plan.

Complementing the almond contemporary cabinets, appliances, floor, and splashboard tile is a delightful abstract wallcovering with dashes of aqua, blue, and pink. The window treatments bring together mini-blinds, topped with a simple valance of a textured cotton fabric in a wavy pattern. An uphostered chair and seat cushions in the same fabric soften the room's straight lines.

What a delightfully informal area for cooking and eating in, whether alone, *a deux,* or with favorite friends.

Changing Times

Over the years tastes change. What was once considered lovely, one day appears old and out of date. When the owners originally decorated their charming French mansard roof home, earth tones were very popular, and as a young family with five small children, they found those colors quite suitable to their lifestyle.

With the children grown, and a whole new palette of colors to choose from, they devised a light, bright scheme for their eat-in kitchen. Beginning with the floor and the terrace beyond the sliding glass doors, white tile and brick bring sparkle to this area. Dark wood cabinets and white countertops remain, while a new delicate blue and white mini-leaf pattern wallpaper replaces the gold walls.

Dated casement draperies were removed to make way for a cheerful garden print in shades of pink, blue, and green. A great example of how you convert old furnishings into something fashionable is the makeover of their dining set. Once gold and black, the table and chairs with their new white marbleized finish and seat cushions to match the wallpaper, give them a new lease on life.

Changing colors sparked this room's refreshing new look, and the family's renewed enjoyment of its kitchen.

Cooking in Style

Large enough to accommodate more than one cook, this gleaming kitchen houses the most up-to-date features. It was designed by Atlanta, Georgia, builder Sue Hillin for her own family. With its glorious dining area, it has become the most lived-in room of the Hillen home.

White paneled cabinets are contrasted with dark green marble countertops. The cooking island is set in a dark band on a floor of white tile squares. Black-front appliances increase the dramatic impact of this dark and light scheme. Gentle sea green balloon shades installed below leaded glass panels bring a soft touch to the room, as does the sophisticated wallpaper.

With the picture of the dining area, you have a preview of what is to come in the final chapter, where you'll be able to see all of this magnificent home.

Chapter 7
Family Room Originals

The term family room signifies warmth and comfort—a cozy room where people are relaxed and carefree. Generally it's a multi-purpose room for watching your favorite TV show, reading the Sunday newspaper, playing games, or just romping with the dog.

It's the ideal room to display your personal treasures, like the railroad memorabilia collector you'll read about next. Family rooms are perfect for exhibiting favorite photos and special awards and trophies. Built-in shelves provide a handsome and practical way to house cherished books and accessories.

Originality knew no limits when it came to the expressive decorating of these dream family rooms.

All Aboard!

Displaying and enjoying their collection of railroad memorabilia was the ultimate goal of this Oklahoma couple, Phil and Laura Judkins, when they began redecorating their family room. The various items had been scattered throughout their home; now they wanted to bring the collection together in one area.

By choosing a single pattern and color—a bold check in pullman green—for wallcovering, upholstery, and window treatment, the room was given a unifying element. With the tie-back draperies the Judkins were able to see out the window, but the cafe curtain hid the sleep sofa from the street.

Some stored away pieces of furniture that have special meaning for the Judkins have found a new home. A trunk that was discovered in the attic is now used as a coffee table, and the inherited rocker makes a great extra seat. Some wonderful old lanterns have been made into lamps. Going back several generations is a marvelous antique display cabinet that was moved from another room. It turned out to be the perfect place to show part of their extensive collection of railroad memorabilia.

Phil installed the wall shelf that now holds his old train set and other treasured mementos. When Laura and Phil come home at night and head for their comfortable TV room, they always enjoy seeing their collection on display.

Rich Mahogany Reflects Tradition

Builder Rob Myers designed a formal family room when he built his own home. The exquisite detailing of the rich mahogany built-in cabinets and bookcases is repeated around the brick fireplace, while fine moulding accents the handsome windows. To keep the room from being too dark, Rob carried the paneling a third of the way up the other walls, leaving the space above white and trimming the ceiling in dark crown moulding.

When planning the interior decorating, Phyllis Myers introduced subtle colors that blend well with the rich mahogany paneling. Simple treatments grace the windows but allow the light to shine in. Traditional fabrics and furnishings round out the rich, classic look.

Working together Phyllis and Rob have created a warm and comfortable family room that works well for entertaining, or being with their children, or for their private moments alone together.

A 1912 House Gets a New Family Room Addition

Interior decorator Barbara Andrews and her family live in a house built in 1912. They moved out of their home for one year while it was being totally renovated and a family room was being added. Barbara and Dickie Andrews wanted their new room to look as if it had always been a part of the original house.

They had the wide mouldings painstakingly matched to those in the original house. On an antiquing expedition for flooring, the Andrewses found the heart of pine boards that truly capture the spirit of the house. Working around some of their cherished antiques, like her mother-in-law's pie safe, Barbara brought in a fresh array of fabrics in cherry pinks, leaf greens, and ocean blues. By changing the fabric to a large, bright floral, detailing the cushions in contrast welting, and adding a few ruffled pillows, she was able to give a tired sofa a brand new look.

The simple swagged and knotted valances over the windows and doors leave the handsome moulding uncovered, and the crisp white mini-blinds allow regulation of the natural light. A matching plaid fabric was used for seat cushions on the antique chairs at the breakfast table. The dhurrie rug has all the bright colors of the fabrics and the same floral motif.

No one would guess that this room was not always a part of the house. Only the decorator and her family know that this charming room is the new addition.

California Country

I t took two years to build Patt and Richard Ross' dream home. Situated in a California canyon, the house has an exterior architectural style that resembles a typical midwestern farmhouse. Interior features and open, vaulted spaces give it a warm California country feeling.

Extravagant use of pine throughout the house is best illustrated in the Rosses' inviting family room. Complementing the light wood tone is a print fabric in a dark forest green. Simple curtains, cushions, and pillows create a cozy window area. "We wanted a welcoming, informal room where our children and grandchild could always feel comfortable," says Patt.

The years of patience and hard work that went into building and decorating their home will give Patt and Richard a lifetime of pleasure to share lovingly with their family.

Light, Bright Space

Family rooms never seem to have sufficient space—you always need more seating and more space for paraphernalia. At the end of a busy day each member of the family should be able to unwind in his or her favorite spot. Whether watching the nightly TV news, catching up on reading, or talking over the events of the day, everyone should be doing it in the most comfortable and carefree room in the house.

The delightfully decorated family room of Terrance and Monica Stein appears larger than it really is. Careful furniture placement and using the light, bright "summer" colors of Monica's own palette create a sense of spaciousness. Building in bookcases and cabinets took up little floor area in return for a lot of storage space. Besides enhancing the fireplace wall, the shelves provide a place for displaying books and accessories. The cabinets hide the TV and the usual conglomeration of games, magazines, and general clutter.

A glass-top coffee table, a pair of low benches, and an armless upholstered chair help to expand the room visually. Painting the interior of the bookcases a dark, rich green that matches the hearth tile adds depth and contrast. The same green is used to border a white area rug.

Continuing the light and airy look, walls and window treatments repeat the sandy white color of the rug, and "summer" pinks and corals brighten the upholstery and pillows. It's the ideal welcoming retreat for the Steins to come home to.

Personal Style

To coordinate with the newly remodeled kitchen, the adjoining intimate family room was treated to the same fresh new colors and patterns. After years of earth tones, the owners find the bright, light color very inviting.

To brighten the dark paneled walls, they selected a cheerful garden print to reupholster the two tuxedo arm sofas. The charming blue and white mini-leaf print graces the window and ruffled throw pillows. Replacing the gold wall-to-wall carpet is a luxurious porcelain blue and white bordered area rug.

This gracious family room is enhanced by precious accesories and books that express the owners' personal style.

Rosy Resort

For two people who spend most of their time traveling on business, being at home is truly a luxury. Sharon and Michael Fields, owners of a large construction and shoring company, decided to turn their California house into a relaxing retreat. Pulling ideas from the various places they have visited, from Key Largo to Phoenix, they created their own rosy resort.

The Fieldses wanted a total change from the heavy earth tones of their family room. They desired a look that would be both sophisticated and soothing. Once they located the variegated pink marble, the tone of the decorating was set. Carrying the floor marble up the fireplace wall to the mantle added depth and created a sumptuous focal point.

Rearranging and recovering their tropical-style wicker furniture lightened up and visually expanded the once crowded-looking room. The selection of a transitional floral in tones of rose and gray also added to brightening and opening up the space. Simple and elegant swagged valances were teamed with pleated shades for the corner window treatment.

The Fieldses wanted an area rug, but did not want to lose the spacious feeling created by the marble floor, so they had a custom rug designed to simulate the pattern and color of the marble. A large, bulky coffee table has been replaced with individual end tables. One shown is a sand-colored rattan haystack-style table.

Green plants in sand-colored planters with matching lamps, and a few well-chosen accessories, complete the Fieldses' tropical pink paradise.

"Eightysomething"...
When You're Young at Heart

Scenic Carmel, California, is the home of a charming and accomplished couple, Robert Walsh and his wife, the former actress, Margaret "Marcy" Walsh. During their long and exciting life they have traveled throughout Europe, England, and North Africa. In the fifties they spent five glorious years living abroad.

Now settled in a new home in Carmel, Margaret is working on her second novel, and has recently had an exhibit of her oil paintings. A former engineering representative for an aircraft company, Robert built the handsome mantel and wonderful English planters that grace their home.

Over the years the Walshes have narrowed down the possessions of a lifetime to only those that hold a special place in their heart. One of those cherished things is a portrait of the glamorous Marcy when she was in her thirties. A new and prized acquistion, a wonderful picture of whales, set the color direction for the cheerful striped fabric. Used for the tailored window draperies and valance, the stripe was also cleverly made into a canopy for the mirrored bar.

White linen sofas and chairs continue the comfortable California chic feeling of this cozy den. Some great-grandparents might find the Walshes updated decorating style too modern for their taste, but for Margaret and Robert being "eightysomething" means nothing when you're young at heart.

Chapter 8
Special Rooms for VSP *(Very Special People)*
. . . Guest Rooms, Children's Rooms

Beginning with a delightful nursery awaiting the arrival of a new baby to the smashing suite for grandmother, all of the rooms in this section were decorated with VSPs in mind. These rooms were lovingly and thoughtfully pulled together to welcome children and grandchildren, friends, parents, and—in the dramatic study, and the hunting lodge bedroom—husbands.

For each of these rooms, providing warmth and comfort was the decorating guideline; making them exceptionally beautiful was the result. The often neglected guest rooms were thoughtfully planned to provide a home away from home for the weary traveler. The importance of children's environments is lovingly shown in the joyous decorating of their individual spaces. And the stunning den is a fine example of the care and attention given a VSH, very special husband.

We hope the rooms for VSPs shown on the following pages will inspire you to do something about your "other bedrooms" . . . those rooms that can be overlooked so easily in the interior decorating scheme of things.

For a Glamorous Grandmother

A globetrotting grandmother's love of Oriental design was the inspiration for this glamorous suite. When she comes to visit her daughter in Colorado, she feels pampered and appreciated in this grandest of rooms.

The imperial dragon-inspired fabric in light hues of lavender, teal green, and jade on a neutral background is echoed in deeper tones with the plum paisley print. Shimmering lavender textured string wallcovering adds to the luxurious feeling. Setting the bed at an angle, the curved canopy, and the flowing drapery give the sleeping area a regal look.

An inviting chaise is positioned so grandmother can enjoy the restful view of the Japanese tea garden. Her daughter has thoughtfully provided a desk and chair for letter writing, and the beautifully carved French armoire for storage or to hold cherished mementos.

Personal attention to detail, such as the contrast banding on the dust ruffle, drapery tie-backs, and the bed pillows, is what makes this suite the perfect setting for a very favorite grandmother.

Dark and Daring

Converting a son's bedroom to a guest room became quite a daring adventure. The first giant step, changing from safe earth tones to dark and dramatic colors led to this striking transition.

Black onyx, emerald green, and ruby red are the fabulous jewel tones used to bring sophisticated appeal to this room. The bed and window treatments are done in a feminine rose and vine floral chintz with accents of masculine black and green check. A classic wing chair also sports the bold check.

The black patterned wallpaper and border is complemented by the plush emerald carpet. Dark colors are carefully mixed with the light tones of the new pine furniture. Brass headboards and accessories heighten the drama of this stunning and welcoming guest room.

One of the owner's long-staying guests has been her son, who has taken up residence in his old room.

Make Yourself at Home

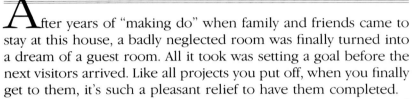

fter years of "making do" when family and friends came to stay at this house, a badly neglected room was finally turned into a dream of a guest room. All it took was setting a goal before the next visitors arrived. Like all projects you put off, when you finally get to them, it's such a pleasant relief to have them completed.

The room's cozy proportions set the mood for an informal country cottage look. Following through on that feeling, the chosen fabric was a floral with an overall diamond rope pattern, predominantly blue on an ivory background with accents of rose. This fabric was used not only for comforters, pillow shams, and the window seat, but covered all of the walls and doors as well. There was no matching wallpaper, but fabric was the preferable choice anyway. It would insure the same color dye, and the plaster walls of the 1896 house would have required a lot of preparation before hanging paper.

A mini-print in blue was made into dust ruffles, the trim on the shams, and to continue the mood, the balloon shades for the three windows. The insides of the closets were covered in the mini-print, and both patterns were combined for the accent pillows.

Deep rose was the choice for the carpet. Sheets and desk accessories in rose tie that color into the rest of the room. In planning the patterns and colors, the plan was to distribute them throughout the space. Wicker furniture in a nutmeg finish completes the romantic country look.

The room is uncluttered, but with enough amenities to say, "Welcome."

Parfait Colors Flavor Guest Suite

The reaction to Becky and Dale Gifford's new guest suite has been, "Wow!" Their whole home has a warm and loving feeling, but when friends see the Giffords' newly decorated addition, they can't help hoping for an invitation to spend a night in the guest room.

The cool parfait colors of peach and mint create a soothing background, while the delicate transitional floral fabric continues the restful mood. Becky fell in love with the sheeting fabric that was used on the two twin beds and at the window. The result is a charming sweep of chintz-lined sheeting across a covered rod for a simply spendid window treatment. When privacy is needed, peach pleated shades can be pulled down.

Matching bolsters and coordinating pillows enhance the bed and make it suitable for daytime lounging. A delicate wallpaper border draws attention to the vaulted ceiling and gracefully arched window. Carpet and walls in the refreshing mint green create a cocoon feeling. The light and airy white rattan furniture carries out the summery look.

The Giffords' love of family and friends is definitely not in words only . . . All you have to do is see this "Wow!" of a guest room to know that.

Southern Hospitality

Norma Young and her husband, Floyd, wanted to provide the visitors who would stay in the guest room of their home with a restful and welcoming atmosphere. "Be a little daring and go with navy blue," was the advice given to Norma. At first she felt apprehensive about using such a dark color, but when the room was finished she knew she had made the right choice.

The guest room continues the contemporary feeling of the rest of the house. Peach PVC vertical blinds with a thin white stripe give the room a tropical mood, which is further enhanced by the ceiling fan. Softening the window treatment is a simple cotton valance, hung with velcro, over the verticals. The valance fabric is repeated on the wide edge of the elegant scalloped headboard.

With the daring splash of navy across the bed, the room turned from merely pretty to dashingly beautiful. By decorating in the striking contrast of soft beige and peach with dark blue, and by a careful blending of the fanciful and the tailored, the room was made appealing to guests of both genders.

Thoughtfully added at the foot of the bed were ottomans to hold luggage or the bedspread. The lounging ceramic cat sets the restful tone for this charming guest refuge.

Going to Grandmother's House

What was once just a spare bedroom has been transformed into a guest room. Not just any guest room, mind you, but one for a very special grandson.

Something warm and comfortable, yet striking and masculine, were the standards that grandmother set for decorating this room. A southwestern pattern in desert colors of teal, clay, and sand blends well with the contemporary light oak furniture.

Framing the window is a fabric-covered lambrequin installed over two-inch wood blinds. Teal cotton tailored skirt and pillows add sparkle to the outline quilted coverlet.

Decorated, but understated, the room is a relaxing haven. Going to grandmother's house is a special treat for her always welcome grandson.

A Beautiful Nest for Bringing Up Baby

This sunny little room in Michigan awaits the arrival of the newest member of the family. Small in size, but prepared lovingly, the nursery is full of the necessary items for bringing up baby.

All set for being the center of attention is the delicate white iron and brass Victorian crib in the middle of the room. A delicate canopied ensemble adorns the crib, while matching pillows decorate the all-important rocker. White wicker furniture will hold new baby's clothes and toys.

Banana yellow carpet sets the pastel tone of the room, and makes it suitable for either a girl or boy. White eyelet curtains are laced with green, yellow, and pink satin ribbons, while stenciled ribbons and bows border the ceiling and the window.

The contented picture is complete with stuffed bears, arms open, ready to welcome baby. What a beautiful beginning for the new little prince or princess!

Room to Grow

Remembering how quickly their son outgrew his nursery, Cindy and Jeff Newman wanted a room for their newborn daughter, Michelle, that would "grow" with her. The plan was to decorate a room that later could be converted easily into a teen room. But for now it is a heavenly place for just being a baby.

Little sheep now jump around the room on a wallpaper border installed at baby's eye level. One day when Michelle is older, the border can easily be changed to something more appropriate. Pink is the traditional color for a girl's room, but for Michelle, it is the sweetly sophisticated combination of mint green and white with touches of pink.

The juxtaposition of straight and curved lines gives this room variety and interest. Relaxing stripes are used in the wallpaper and repeated in the cotton coverlet, while the white and gold French Provincial furniture adds lovely, softly curved lines. Lucky Michelle gets to grow up with the same cherished furniture her mother had as a child.

A luxurious deep pile peacock-colored carpet is the perfect place for baby to learn to crawl. The canopy bed and the puffed valance are dressed in a soft green and white dotted fabric. Alongside the stuffed sheep and toys, Cindy added an array of ruffled pillows, as well as stiffened bows which appear at the corner of the room and are also used as picture hangers.

Growing up in such a beautifully conceived room can't help but pique Michelle's interest in a career in interior decorating!

Today's Child

Suzanne Thomas, the bright four-year-old resident of this chic little California room, expressed an interest in contemporary decorating. That was not so unusual, given the fact that when her parents moved to a city townhouse, they went from country to contemporary. Betty Thomas adds that her daughter is an independent thinker, and even at her young age knows what she wants.

Sleek two-toned furniture is scaled for a child, but provides ample space for Suzanne's growing needs. A simple shutter treatment covers the one large window, while draperies were used to create a tailored canopy treatment for the bed. In keeping with the spare, straight lines of the room, the mattress is wrapped in a channel quilted, fitted coverlet. For a soft, feminine touch, a subtle striped floral fabric and bow details were added.

Betty decorated her daughter's room in summer colors so that Suzanne would enjoy being in it. The creamy pat o' butter yellow, peach, and white color scheme with leafy green accents gives Suzanne a sunny California contemporary space just like Mommy's.

For Someone Special

Ask any teen-age girl what she would like most when her family moves to a new house and you will probably hear ... "my own room ... pretty and feminine ... decorated in my favorite colors." There's a girl in Arkansas who got all three of those wishes.

An active high school freshman, Lara Collins has her very own dream room to come home to. As pretty and lovely as she is, the room not only is decorated in Lara's two favorite colors of blue and peach, but it has been done by her favorite interior decorator, her grandmother. From the beginning it was a labor of love for both.

The charming cotton stripe fabric with delicate lilies of the valley was used for the coverlet, pillow shams, and gently gathered and tied back window treatments. A blue mini-floral coordinate is made into the dust ruffle and pillows. Walls are painted peach and have a wallpaper border at the ceiling.

"I loved taking these soft colors and gentle patterns and creating this lovely bedroom because I was doing it for someone special," proclaims the proud grandmother.

Quiet Place

One woman's loving gesture was to decorate a unique room for her husband. His den, viewed from the second floor balcony, shows a quiet area for writing or reading, or for his favorite hobby, chess. Sophisticated, but inviting, the lush room was created around a warm color scheme of desert pinks and peaches, turquoise and teal.

Subtle colorations in the grasscloth wallcovering provide a serene background. The knotted and draped asymmetric window treatment gracefully accents the arched window, while a tricolor area rug repeats the arch motif. Cactus and desert-type plants in terra cotta containers complete the southwestern feeling.

The wall not shown is lined with bookcases, which add another dimension to one man's very special quiet place.

Room with a View

What makes this room so special is that it was decorated for the Maryland Eastern Shore hunting lodge of a very special person . . . my husband, Jim. He provided me with the new wing to our old log cabin, and I decorated the romantic master bedroom for him.

The focal point of the room is the pewter and brass French four-poster bed, set at an angle to take advantage of our glorious river view. Draped in lace and strewn with branches of ivy, the bed is outfitted with a plump down comforter over a feather bed.

Four coordinating prints were chosen in a serene color scheme of soothing shades of green and blue, and rose pink. The delicate floral wallcovering and border with a sky blue background enhances the view.

The major investment in the room is the four-poster bed, but everyone has a budget. I found the dresser and the night table at a second-hand store, and I painted them and then antiqued both pieces my favorite sea green color.

Two hand-me-down chairs, originally in a khaki fabric, were recovered, and a ruffled skirt added to soften the look. The night table is a simple plywood thirty-inch round and thirty-inch high table with a flowing skirt. Behind the bed is a painted leather folding screen to accent the empty corner.

For the sake of privacy and insulation there are textured pleated shades at the windows and doors. Framing both are yards of bordered lace. Lace is wonderful to work with because you don't have to line it, and in this instance there was no sewing. The lace was cut, left unhemmed, and just puddled on the floor. Pulled through brass rings, it literally took minutes to install. This simple window treatment gives our bedroom a pleasing, uncontrived look that carries out perfectly the informal country feeling.

Remember, decorating a room is more than selecting colors and fabrics. It involves creating a mood and making a room comfortable and inviting with a loving touch. It's easy when when you're doing it for a VSH.

Chapter 9
Bathing Beauties . . . Bathrooms

No more just little necessary rooms, luxurious bathrooms have become one of the most desirable areas in a house. With the advent of jacuzzis and the return of soaking tubs, unhurried and relaxing bathing is a wish come true.

Each of the bathrooms shown here has been cleverly turned into a lush mini-spa. Beautiful fabrics and wallcoverings set the sybaritic mood. Some are soothing, others dramatic, but they are always suited to the individual's need to be pampered.

These imaginative colors and designs should inspire a bathing beauty of your very own.

Bathing in Luxury

A large window, high ceilings, and white walls made this bathroom cold and uninviting. Virginia Sutherland wanted to warm up the space so she would feel comfortable, and pampered. Finding the ethereal wallcovering was the first step toward attaining her deluxe bathroom.

The dusty rose cloud-like vinyl wallcovering accented with gold metallic makes a soothing and flattering background for the room. Around the tall window, with its wispy floral motif stained glass panels, is a subtle flamestitch print. The lavish rose-colored soaking tub is trimmed in tile with gentle flowers.

Warm hues and serene patterns have converted this once bland and cold space into the luxurious and comfortable bathroom that Virginia had envisioned.

Mirror, Mirror on the Wall

With the extravagant use of mirrors, this narrow bathroom has been given the perception of increased width. Using mirrors over the long vanity and on the closet doors has visually tripled the space. It is now a joy for Californians Steve and Barbara Coffey to be in their bright and cheery bathroom.

The mirror magic is enhanced further by Barbara's selection of cool blue and warm peach, which repeats the colors of the master bedroom. More privacy was given to the window by adding a cafe curtain over the semi-sheer pleated shade. The soft blue is echoed in the wallcovering. Both colors are sharpened by the crisp white of the tile, countertop, and the trim.

Mirror, mirror on the wall, who's the fairest of them all? This beauty of a bathroom, of course!

Classic Cool

Sleek and cool was what Myra Munn and her husband, Aubrey, wanted for their bathroom. When they moved into their new home they finally got the bathroom of their dreams.

Creamy white with pale peach creates the classic background. Two sinks, plenty of storage space, and a special vanity area for Myra are just the beginning of the luxurious appointments. Add to those gold-plated fixtures, recessed lighting, and large expanses of mirror. The splashy flowers of the wallcovering contrast nicely with the sleek lines of the cabinetry.

A terra cotta Greek god approvingly surveys this classically cool master bath.

Beautiful Reflections

Lavishly mirrored walls reflect the Hillins' beautiful master bathroom. Dramatically designed by builder Sue Hillin for her own home, this room continues the excitement and rich colors of the rest of the house.

Because Sue wanted to coordinate the bath with her master bedroom, the plan was to paper the walls in a matching wallcovering. When none was available, fabric was painstakingly installed in its place. As it sometimes turns out in decorating, the Hillens love the softness of the fabric played against the stark white tile and cabinets, and the sparkling mirrors.

The last word in bathrooms has to be the sumptuous green marble tub located below a leaded glass window. Sue's attention to detail shows here in her corner block treatments to the crown moulding, and the pilasters at the window.

Alluring Arrangement

Next to Phyllis and Rob Myers' chic country master bedroom is their luxurious bathroom. Neatly arranged, it combines blush pink with sophisticated black and gray for dramatic impact.

An interesting floor plan with angled walls gives a feeling of elegance and spaciousness. Over the tub an arched window with its fan-pleated shade creates the room's exciting focal area. Painting the ceiling pink is a surprising touch.

The bright white floor and trim heightens the visual impact of the Myerses alluring master bathroom.

Mint Fresh

Adjacent to the guest room in their new addition is a spacious bathroom. Becky and Dale Gifford wanted to provide visitors to their gracious Texas home with privacy and comfort. In the new luxurious guest suite everyone feels pampered.

The same dreamy colors of the bedroom flow into the bathroom. A refreshing mint and peach abstract stripe wallcovering lights up the space, and crisp white cabinets, fixtures, and trim continue the bright and airy feeling. Peach tiles are used both on the countertop and the floor.

Sparkling aqua towels, white wicker, and peach knobs add the finishing touches to this carefully decorated room.

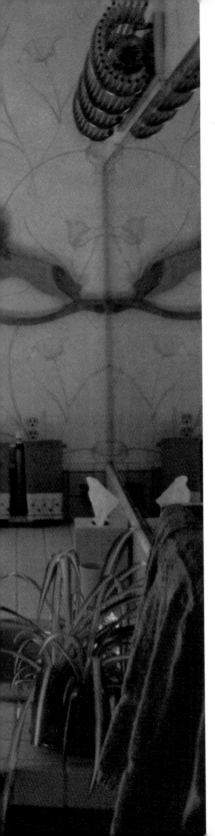

Canyon View

This fun-loving California couple, Diane and Malcolm Sagen-kahn, wanted to decorate their bathroom. What they didn't want was to cover up their glorious view of the canyon.

Privacy was not a factor, so a simple balloon valance was used just to soften the tall windows and the high ceilings. A wallcovering with splashes of pink and blue matches the valance. The soft, neutral colors of the room provide a nondistracting background and a wonderful, soothing feeling.

The Sagenkahns have a beautifully decorated bathroom and an uninterrupted view of their fabulous canyon.

Splendor in the Bath

To coordinate with the owners' dramatic adjoining master bedroom, this bathroom was given the same high contrast color scheme. The corner angled tub sets the stage for the room's dramatic decorating.

A transitional floral dots the black vinyl wallcovering, and tiles in sand with black stripes accent the white tub area. Cotton swags in sand, lined in white and draped over black poles, combine the three dominant colors, and add softness and drama to the room. White duettes at the windows tie in beautifully with the white fixtures.

Elegant accessories combining silver and gold add the finishing touches to this splendid master bathroom.

Chapter 10
Window Wizardry

Each window presents its own unique challenge; and more often than not, there are many alternative solutions that would work equally well. Before designing a window treatment here are four questions that you should ask to help you determine an appropriate solution:

1. Do I need to cover the window totally because of an unpleasant view or for privacy?
2. Do I need special insulation protection because of climate or lack of storm windows?
3. Which direction does the window face . . . sun or shade?
4. Aesthetically, what treatment will work best with the rest of the room's decorating direction?

One common mistake that people often make is to leave a window bare because of a beautiful view. They forget that when the sun goes down, the window area can become a black hole. At night even a simple treatment framing the window will add warmth to the room. Pleated shades or mini-blinds that retract all the way afford a daytime view with nighttime privacy.

Highlight

The challenge presented by the windows in this condominium was to come up with something different as well as practical to cover the atrium door and adjacent window, while allowing for an unobstructed view of the ocean. Dramatic but simply swagged treatments provided a serenely elegant solution. The proportions of the swags and jabots have been adjusted to fit the two different size window areas.

Peach fabric-covered poles and lining offer a rich contrast to the deep green cotton of the swag. The special detail of adding a second pole to the door treatment enhances the elegant look.

Apple Blossom Time

A light and airy look was desired for the six windows of this sublime master bedroom. "Keep the windows clear of fabric, yet retain my privacy and block out the morning sun," was the directive of the homeowner.

Working around the Oriental apple blossom theme of the stained glass and the area rug, a delicate version of a blossoming branch is painted on the wall. A lustrous fabric is swagged asymmetrically across the window and gracefully falls to the floor. Blockout roller shades hidden under this treatment take care of sun and privacy.

This elegant corner evokes the cool serenity associated with the Orient.

French Country Corner

Aunique window treatment transformed this average window into a an elegant backdrop for the breakfast area of this kitchen. Counterpointing the curves of the French country furniture is the tailored lambrequin that frames the double window.

The uncluttered design of the space and the geometric floral pattern is classic French in feeling. A matching shade is held with contrasting ties. Underneath, but not visible is a roller shade. Using the same diamond pattern fabric on the chairs completes this French country corner.

Braided Reflections

Braiding solid fabric colors that reflect the tones of the sofas was the striking solution to the wall of sliding glass doors in this Florida home. By simply accenting the window, and leaving an uninterrupted view of the pool and the palm trees, the living space was visually expanded.

For installation, the unique braid treatment can be affixed with velcro to a cornice board. How you vary the colors of the cords will depend on which colors you want to empasize. If you want to highlight one color, just increase the number of cords of that color.

The picture of this room at night provides a good illustration of how even windows with great views need some kind of a treatment to soften them after the sun goes down. To add another area of interest to the window without taking away from the scenery, a shelf was installed above the the braid to hold a basket collection.

Dual Treatment

This austere bathroom window over the tub was warmed up visually and given better proportions by dividing the space in half. Two narrow hard cornices relieve the vertical lines and with the soft side panels, frame the windows. The serene flamestitch print fabric picks up the blue grays and rose pinks of the stained glass windows.

Upper and lower sections of the window each have their own mini-blind. The dual handling of this window allows for a variety of light and privacy situations. Whatever way the minis are moved now the bather has a beautiful view.

Different Design

The owners of this Michigan home wanted unusual treatments that would balance the atrium doors and windows with the room's large dimensions, while keeping it simple and functional. A combination of soft valances and drapery side panels, pleated shades, and vertical blinds blend with the classic colors of coral, French blue, and ecru.

Short vertical blinds cover the dining area bay window, and pleated shades hang on the atrium doors. Tying them together are intricate valances and panels in a subtle floral with triangular insets of blue. This unique design sets the soothing style for this much-lived-in room.

Updated Look Unifies Windows

It was time to update and glamorize the various windows in this room. The woven wood shades in earth tones had worn well, but now a brighter, newer look was in order.

From the wide variety of choices available today, a toasty beige pleated shade was selected to unify the windows and doors. This neat, clean look was enhanced further by an abstract cotton print in cool blues and warm, rosy beige. Simple side panels were topped with softly gathered valances on continental rods. The tapered treatment of the valances not only provides a gracious design element, but allows for easy door clearance.

For all its practicality, the beauty of this updated look is in the way it renews appreciation of this charming room.

Layered Look

The only windows in this Massachusetts master bedroom were treated to a lovely layered look. Working with a restful color combination of dusty blues and mauves, a transitional floral was chosen for balloon shades and soft valances. The shades, mounted inside the dark-stained window frame, can be raised to let in the light, or pulled down for complete darkness.

Raising the shade halfway and having a delicate rose-patterned white lace shirred on rods below allows for both privacy and light. The quilted valance with gracefully curved contrast edging, mounted on a board above the window frame, adds the finishing touch to the treatment. Notice the mirror with the matching fabric gathered around the frame.

Summery Stripes

A vibrant cotton stripe in seashore colors of aqua, coral, and sand tops off the kitchen window in this home. Designed to be purely decorative and eye catching, the treatment is deceptively simple. The striped fabric is pleated and drawn up by two adjustable aqua ties fitted under the solid aqua hard cornice that is outlined in contrast welting. Not seen, but available if privacy is required, is a mini-blind drawn up behind the treatment.

A Warm Feeling

The lovely drapery treatment in this dining room leaves touches of the handsome wood frame exposed. Irish lace panels give privacy, but let the light shine in. The traditional theme of the home was carried through in the choice of a cotton chintz in the jewel tones of ruby and emerald and accents of topaz. Large, soft knots tie the drapery and valance together. Contrasting red banding at the hem adds a final detail.

Chapter 11
Builder's Showstopper House

The spectacular Atlanta home of Sue and Bob Hillin is the culmination of builder/owner Sue's experiences building custom houses for other people. A few years back, she decided that it was time for her family to enjoy the kind of luxurious home she had been designing for others. From the splendid Southern facade to the dramatic interiors, Sue created a showstopper of a house.

Sue Hillin's trademark of special attention to detail is immediately apparent on seeing the grand staircase. Her innate sense of scale and proportion carries through to every area of the house. Ceilings are usually the most neglected part of a home, but not when Sue is building. "Everyone emphasizes floors and walls, and then totally neglects the ceiling. I think a room is incomplete if the ceiling is left plain." Look up when you enter the Hillin residence and you'll see exquisitely designed and paneled detail.

Another of Sue's marks is her unusual treatment of windows. Often her designs incorporate one of her favorite materials, leaded glass. Telling us about her interest in rich wood paneling and custom cabinetry, like that shown in the library, Sue says, "These are two important elements that help to personalize a house to fit the needs of the people who use the rooms."

What has to be one of the loveliest areas of the house is the large eat-in kitchen. It is almost two separate areas, one housing the most up-to-date kitchen features, and the other a breakfast room as crisp and fresh as an early spring morning.

Wicker furniture was spray-painted to match green marble countertops. Seat cushions and a flowing tableskirt are made out of a glorious garden print in colors of peach tulip and vine green. A two-tone green cotton print is used for the balloon shades and inviting window seat, as well as for a table topper. Walls are covered in a dark mini-print that contrasts nicely with the clean white built-ins and mouldings. Below is a floor of white tile, and above is a charming white chandelier.

This house was obviously planned so that all rooms would be enjoyed and lived in. Especially significant is the way the formal living room is open to the kitchen and breakfast area. Traditional camelback sofas in a flamestitch pattern are matched to the tapered balloon window treatments.

High style and sophistication are the best words to describe Sue and Bob's master bedroom suite. The chiaroscuro effect of arranging light and dark seen throughout the house is most effectively observed here. A blush white background sets off the jewel

tones on black of the chinoiserie-patterned cotton print. Emerald green fabric provides a clear color accent. Using a wallpaper border below the crown moulding brought color and pattern to the ceiling line.

When the coordinating wallpaper was unavailable, fabric was used to cover the bathroom walls. Once again, we see examples of Sue's attention to detail. Lavishly mirrored walls, corner block treatments to the crown moulding, and the pilasters at the custom leaded glass window create an alluring elegance.

The Hillins' children have equally beautiful rooms. Scott's is furnished with a masculine plaid, while Tammy's is every girl's dream of a romantic, feminine bedroom.

Whether together or alone in their personal spaces, this home reflects the loving gift that builder Sue Hillin gave to her family.

Thanks!
Interior Decorators & Photographers

The following is a list by page number of the interior decorators and photographers whose work appears in this book.

Note: **Decorators' names appear in bold.**
Photographers' names appear in italics.

Page 1
Carol Donayre Bugg
Gordon Beall

Pages 2–3
Bobbie J. Haseley
Peter Turo

Pages 20–25
Mary Ann Weakley
Robert Johnson

Pages 26, 28–29
Carol Donayre Bugg
Gordon Beall

Pages 30–31
Mary Ann Weakley
Bill Gutmann

Pages 32–33
Edie Stull
Bob Byrd

Pages 34–35
Sandra Cook
Gillian Randall

Pages 36–37
Carole Ponzio
Gene Remillard

Pages 38–39
Debbie Richerson
Brenda Pequignot
Hank Ercolani

Pages 40–41
Sherry Butterfield
Bob Byrd

Pages 42–43
Anne Fawcett
Paul Constantino

Pages 44–45
Suzanne Claiborne
Karen Montgomery

Pages 46–47
Teri Ervin-Hugo
Bob Bates

Pages 48–49
Carol Stearns
Marcia Tomchay

Pages 50–51
Sondra Stewart
Christopher Weeks

Pages 52–53
Mary Bahar
Michael Landis

Pages 54–55
Necole Querbach
David Ely

Pages 56–59
Fran Graham
Terry Davis

Pages 60–61
Necole Querbach
David Ely

Pages 62–63
Bobbie J. Haseley
Peter Turo

Pages 64–65
Barbara Andrews
Trey Mainwaring

Pages 66–67
Judith Slaughter
Aleta Stratton
Bob Bates

Pages 68–69
Carole Ponzio
Russ Taylor

Pages 70–71
Cindy Schweisthal
John Felix

Pages 146–147
Nancy Davison
Ed Sandlin

Pages 148–149
Debra Porter
Moline Ostlund

Pages 150–151
Mary Vescio
Brian Kurtis

Pages 152–153
Mary Bahar
Michael Landis

Pages 154–155
Karen Montgomery
Karen Montgomery

Pages 156–157
Judy Appel
John Mandeville

Pages 158–159
Dot Bushong
Jim Morris

Pages 160–161
Mary Bahar
Michael Landis

Pages 162–163
Carol Donayre Bugg
Gordon Beall

Page 164
Judith Slaughter
Bob Bates

Pages 166–167
Cindy Schweisthal
John Felix

Pages 168–169
Michele Lewis
Jeffrey Meyers

Pages 170–171
Ed Whitton
Don Blake

Pages 172–173
Judith Slaughter
Bob Bates

Pages 174–175
Terri Ervin-Hugo
Bob Bates

Pages 176–177
Nancy Davison
Ed Sandlin

Pages 178–179
Judy Appel
John Mandeville

Pages 180–181
Mary Bahar
Michael Landis

Pages 182–185
Sheryl Reed
Paul Constantino

Pages 186–187
Jacqueline Yarmo
Richard Croteau

Pages 188–189
Suzanne Claiborne
Karen Montgomery

Pages 190–191
Carole Ponzio
Russ Taylor

Pages 192–193
Cindy Schweisthal
John Felix

Pages 194–195
Carol Sanborn
Marilyn Slezak

Pages 196–197
Karen Montgomery
Karen Montgomery

Pages 198–199
Linda Risley
Linda Risley

Pages 200–201
Nancy Davison
Ed Sandlin

Pages 202–203
Patricia Lahr
Joseph Lahr

Pages 204–210
Judith Slaughter
Bob Bates

Index

Dream Rooms for Real People

Arrange a free professional consultation with your local Decorating Den owner.

Write to:
Carol Donayre Bugg, ASID
Decorating Den Systems, Inc.
4630 Montgomery Avenue
Bethesda, Maryland 20814
1-800-428-1366

Own a Decorating Den franchise and fulfill your dream . . .

Imagine . . . a fun job that allows you to be creative,
. . . managing your own business and creating your own hours,
. . . working for yourself, but not by yourself.

Join more than 1,000 executives, teachers, physicians, and homemakers who have changed their career paths to become professionally trained Decorating Den franchise owners.

Call 1-800-332-3367 or write to: Carol Donayre Bugg, ASID. Decorating Den Systems, Inc., 4630 Montgomery Avenue, Bethesda, Maryland 20814